M

DATE DUE

PRINTED IN U.S.A.

Veterans Day

ABDO
Publishing Company

A Buddy Book
by
Julie Murray

Buddy BOOKS
Holidays

VISIT US AT
www.abdopublishing.com

Published by ABDO Publishing Company, 8000 West 78th Street, Edina, Minnesota 55439.

Copyright © 2012 by Abdo Consulting Group, Inc. International copyrights reserved in all countries. No part of this book may be reproduced in any form without written permission from the publisher. Buddy Books™ is a trademark and logo of ABDO Publishing Company.

Printed in the United States of America, North Mankato, Minnesota.
052011
092011

 PRINTED ON RECYCLED PAPER

Coordinating Series Editor: Rochelle Baltzer
Editor: Sarah Tieck
Contributing Editors: Megan M. Gunderson, BreAnn Rumsch, Marcia Zappa
Graphic Design: Denise Esner
Cover Photograph: *Shutterstock*: JustASC.
Interior Photographs/Illustrations: *AP Photo*: AP Photo (p. 7), Paul Efird/Knoxville News Sentinel (p. 5), Findlay Kember (p. 9), Martinez Monsivais (p. 17), Susan Walsh (p. 19); *Michael David Novak* (pp. 8, 11, 15, 16, 21, 22); *Shutterstock*: Colette3 (p. 13).

Library of Congress Cataloging-in-Publication Data

Murray, Julie, 1969-
 Veterans Day / Julie Murray.
    p. cm. -- (Holidays)
  ISBN 978-1-61783-043-3
  1. Veterans Day--Juvenile literature. I. Title.
 D671.M87 2012
 394.264--dc22
                            2011002292

Table of Contents

What Is Veterans Day?

Veterans Day happens every year on November 11. It is a national US holiday. Several other countries have comparable holidays.

Veterans are people who have served in the military. Veterans Day honors their service with parades and **ceremonies**.

Many US cities host Veterans Day parades.

5

Beginnings

On November 11, 1918, an **armistice** ended **World War I**. One year later, President Woodrow Wilson wanted to honor US veterans of the war. So, he set aside November 11 as Armistice Day. This honored the end of fighting.

Many countries celebrated the 1918 armistice. This meant their loved ones could come home from war.

Armistice Day became an official US holiday in 1938. **World War II** and the **Korean War** followed. Afterward, Americans wanted to honor veterans of all wars. So in 1954, Armistice Day was renamed Veterans Day.

Veterans from many different wars observe Veterans Day.

In the United Kingdom, Remembrance Day is observed on the second Sunday in November.

Today, several other countries have holidays to honor veterans on or near November 11. In France, people observe **Armistice** Day. In the United Kingdom, Canada, Australia, and New Zealand the holiday is called Remembrance Day.

Time for Peace

The 1918 **armistice** took effect on the eleventh hour of the eleventh day of the eleventh month. So for many people, the number 11 is an important part of Veterans Day. Many Veterans Day **ceremonies** begin at 11 AM.

At most Veterans Day ceremonies, an honor guard brings in flags. This is called presenting the colors.

Red Poppies

During **World War I**, many soldiers fought in Europe. There, plants called corn poppies often grew on battlefields.

In 1915, a poem by Canadian soldier John McCrae was printed. This famous poem is called "In Flanders Fields." It is about the battlefields and the poppies.

Today, red poppies are a **symbol** of World War I and the soldiers who died. They are a common part of Remembrance Day events around the world.

Corn poppies are native to Europe, North Africa, and Asia.

Red, White, and Blue

A flag is a **symbol** of a country. People fly flags near government buildings and homes. During wartime, flags become very important symbols.

When Americans think of Veterans Day, they often think of the US flag. So on this holiday, people carry flags in parades and **ceremonies**.

Each star on the US flag stands for one of the 50 states. Each stripe represents one of the original 13 colonies.

Never Forget

On Veterans Day, some people visit **cemeteries** for veterans. By doing so, they honor people who served the United States.

Being buried in a cemetery for veterans is a special honor.

President Barack Obama has attended the Veterans Day ceremony at Arlington National Cemetery.

Arlington National **Cemetery** is near Washington, D.C. It holds a Veterans Day **ceremony** each year at 11 AM. The US president often attends.

During the **ceremony** at Arlington National **Cemetery**, people honor a special **tomb**. The Tomb of the Unknowns was established on November 11, 1921.

In 1921, the body of a **World War I** soldier was buried there. No one knew who he was. But, they wanted to honor him and others like him. Today, this grave is a **symbol**. It honors all Americans lost in war.

Soldiers guard the Tomb of the Unknowns. Three unknown soldiers are now buried there.

Veterans Day Today

Today, Veterans Day honors all American veterans. On this day, people attend events. They fly the American flag. Some visit **cemeteries** for veterans. They remember the brave people who fought for their country.

On Veterans Day, people honor veterans who have died by visiting their graves.

Interesting Facts

- Some countries honor soldiers who died in **World War I** in a special way. On November 11, people are silent for two minutes at 11 AM.

- In 2010, there were about 23 million living US veterans.

- Long ago, only men were soldiers. In 1948, a law was passed that allowed women to become regular members of the military.

Before they could fight, women worked as nurses or service pilots. Today, they are honored for their service (*right*).

Important Words

armistice a pause in fighting.

cemetery a place where the dead are buried.

ceremony a formal event on a special occasion.

Korean War a war fought in North and South Korea from 1950 to 1953.

symbol (SIHM-buhl) an object or mark that stands for an idea.

tomb (TOOM) a special building or structure that houses the dead.

World War I a war fought in Europe from 1914 to 1918.

World War II a war fought in Europe, Asia, and Africa from 1939 to 1945.

Web Sites

To learn more about Veterans Day,
visit ABDO Publishing Company online. Web sites about Veterans Day are featured on our Book Links page. These links are routinely monitored and updated to provide the most current information available.

www.abdopublishing.com

Index